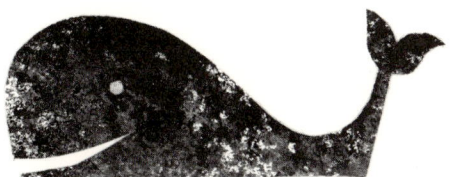

PETER DESBARATS

The Night the City Sang

ILLUSTRATIONS BY
FRANK NEWFELD

McCLELLAND AND STEWART

Revised Edition   COPYRIGHT   ©1977 by McClelland and Stewart Limited

Text copyright   ©1977 by Peter Desbarats

Originally published as *Halibut York & More*

These poems originally appeared in *The Montreal Star*, 1963, 1964, 1965.

ALL RIGHTS RESERVED

McClelland and Stewart Limited,
The Canadian Publishers,
25 Hollinger Road,
Toronto, Ontario.
M4B 3G2

DESIGNED BY FRANK NEWFELD

PRINTED AND BOUND IN CANADA

BY THE HUNTER ROSE COMPANY

CANADIAN CATALOGUING IN PUBLICATION DATA

Desbarats, Peter, 1933-
The night the city sang

First published under title: Halibut York & More.

ISBN 0-7710-2685-4

1. Christmas – Juvenile poetry.   I. Newfeld, Frank, 1928-
II. Title.

PS8507.E72N54 1977   jC811'.5'4   C77-001305-8
PR9199.3.D47N54 1977

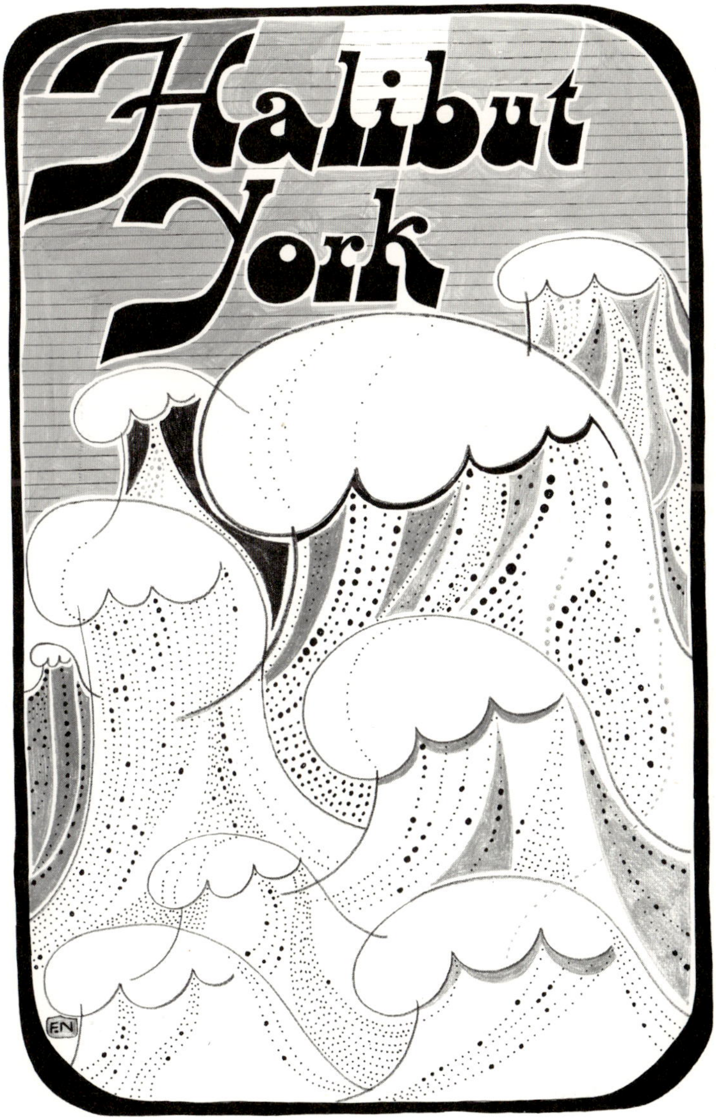
Halibut
York
F.N

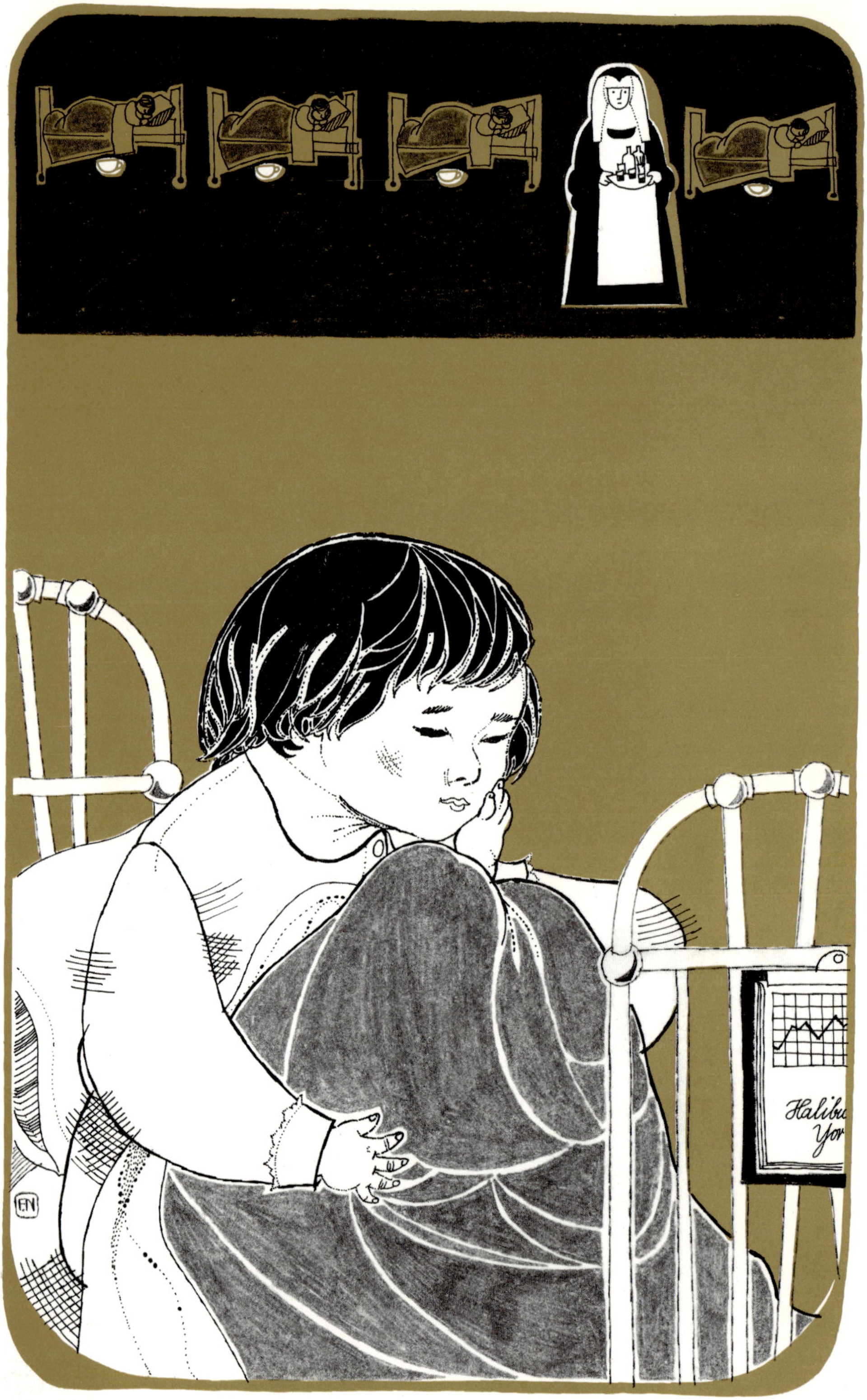

All around her, hospital beds,
Gently-breathing heads, sleighbells
Ringing through their Christmas dreams.
High above Atwater, the children slept
All but Halibut York, who kept
Her knees tucked beneath her chin
Eskimo eyes open wide
Dark as the winter night outside.

She thought of her mother. The house of snow.
The flame dying in the stone bowl.
The dogs howling. The sleigh flying.
Her father crying. The silver bird.
She came to the place where children lie
In sunlit caves beneath the sky.
In moonlit caves the silver children slept
And dark as the night, Halibut York wept.

'God,' she said, 'Santa Claus, Jesus,
'Whichever is right, I want to pray.
'This is my wish: a whale.
'A whale with a necklace of seals and walrus
'With dolphins dangling from his tail,
'A whale for me on Christmas day
'A whale with a back as black as rock
'Send it to Halibut York. Okay?'

God heard, and to Him it wasn't absurd
But what an order! It made Him reel.
How could He beg, borrow or steal
A whale in a week for Halibut York?

He leaned from Heaven, close to the world,
Cast His eye upon the Atlantic,
Placed His ear within the ocean,
Listened for a whale's commotion.
In Hudson Bay, by Baffin Island
Down the coast of Greenland moved the Lord
Of Eskimos and whales.
He found His whale off Reykjavik
And into the tiny, gentle brain
God quietly slipped a notion
That's all it took —
The ocean shook as Mot ascended,
Surfaced — Great Scott — this isn't a whale
It's the British Isles with a glorious tail.

It's insular
Peninsular
It's a nation, a continent, a world!
That's the way Mot looked
Uncurled.

Mot was a lot of whale, but gentle,
Strong as an earthquake, mentally mild,
A mile of child.
He didn't know
Why he wanted to go
Up the St. Lawrence.
It's not the natural habitat
Of whales. Mot knew that.
But his tiny soul flamed with desire
His blubber burned with divine fire
He rose from the sea for a final spout
And then
He was off!
Avast! Look out!

Cruising past the tip of Greenland
He upset an atomic submarine and
Set it aright before he proceeded.
The captain, a tough old salt, needed
A long rest after that.
He had peered through his periscope, seen Mot,
Said, 'Nope . . . it can't be . . . it's not . . .
'It's a whale!' His mate put him to bed.
'The end of a fine career,' he said.

The wake of Mot was a polyglot
Turmoil of seal, porpoise and squid;
The sea boiled as the walrus churned;
Past Newfoundland the procession turned
Into the Gulf of St. Lawrence it slid.
Shark and barracuda bored
Peacefully through the rushing horde
Neglecting their normal stalking of prey.
Electric eels refrained from shocking.

They rushed past Percé.
A solitary curé
Walking one morning by the river
Saw the motley crew
Heading for Rivière-du-Loup.
Warned in advance, La Malbaie
Declared a public holiday.
Thousands lined the northern shore
To marvel at Mot. Never before
(Since Wolfe)
Had there been such an uproar.

The boardwalk at Quebec was packed
With people as Mot squeezed
Under the bridge. He sneezed
As he passed beneath the crowded span.
Everyone ran as the mighty sneezing
Engulfed the bridge in a cloud of freezing
Spray. What a sight!
Gesundheit!

In Montreal, three ocean ships
Were pinned by ice against the slips
Caught by an early winter.
Captains gnashed their teeth
As the ice gnashed beneath
Their bridges, threatening to splinter
The ships to smithereens.

Icebreakers shivered and shook as they plied,
Pried, tried and decided
Nothing could budge the ice 'til spring.
Captains and crews were fit to be tied
When word of Mot reached the riverside.

At Trois Rivières, according to reports,
The whale had met ice. With monstrous snorts
He ground his teeth and thrashed his tail.
For miles around it seemed to hail
As ice flew from the central channel.
Elated
Mot granulated every floe.
Through Lac St. Pierre he flailed a path.
On the roofs of Sorel, the ice cubes rained
Like snow.

On Christmas Eve, triumphant Mot
Entered the harbour of Montreal.
The captains cheered, the whistles blew,
The vessels left – and no one knew
Why the whale, the dolphins and otter
Gathered together at the foot of Atwater
Waited for dawn on Christmas day
And staged an unforgettable display.

Mot blew fountains higher than skyscrapers,
Seals cut capers, porpoise whistled,
With mackerel leaping, flounder flipping,
Walrus trying to dance
On St. Helen's Island
Slipping and roaring with maritime glee.

High above Atwater, Halibut knew
This was her whale, her dolphins,
Her herring, her hullabaloo.

Citizens crowded the harbour to see,
Millions of others watched on TV.
Marine biologists, white from shock,
Tried to count the riotous flock,
Measured Mot from every angle
Whenever they managed to disentangle
His shape from the leaping wreathes of fish.
'It's the Gulf Stream,' they said, 'an aberration,
'It's the atom bomb, it's fluoridation,
'It's austerity, it's creeping inflation.'
And none of them guessed, as they gazed at the fish
It was Halibut York's Christmas wish.

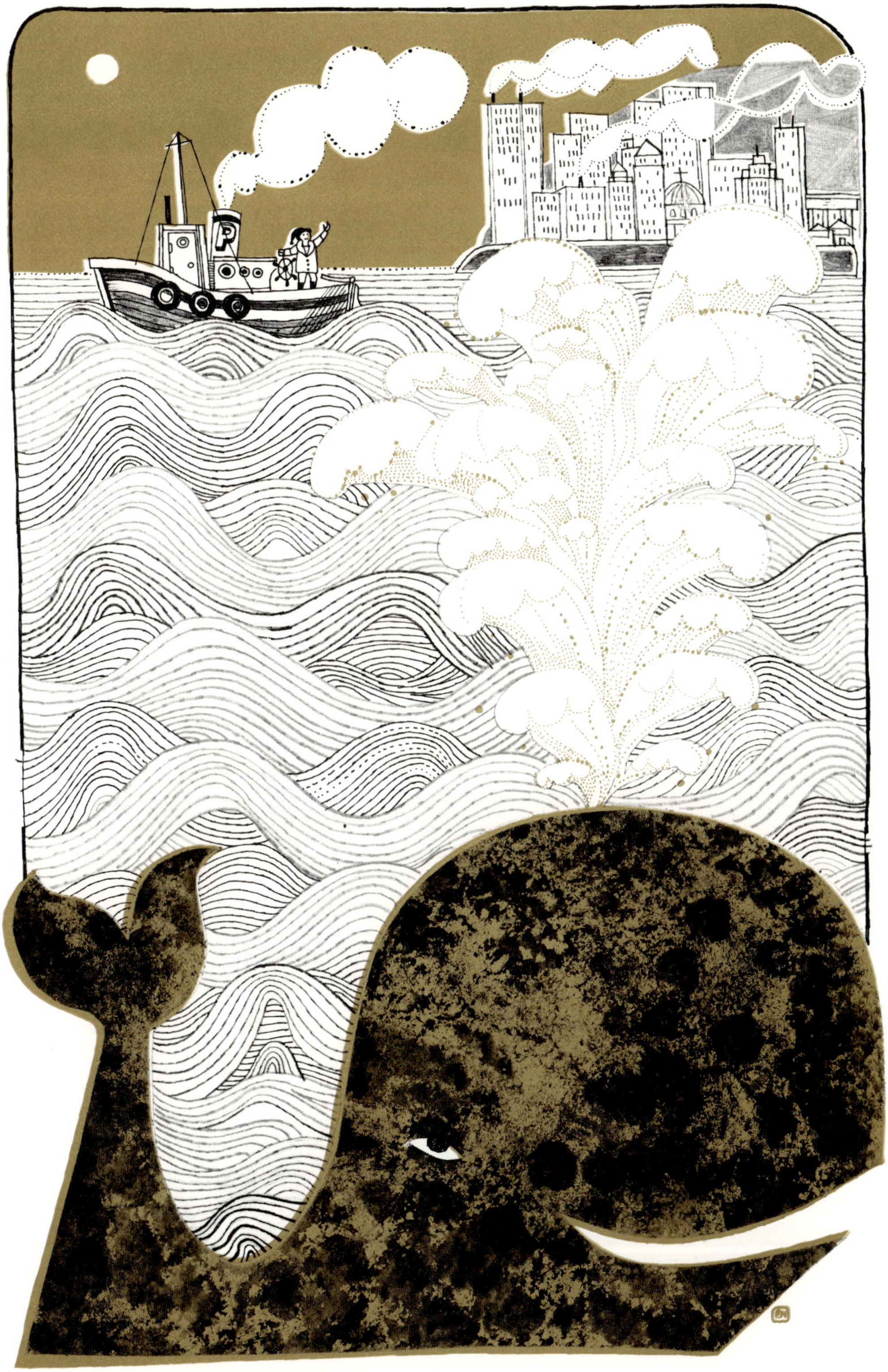

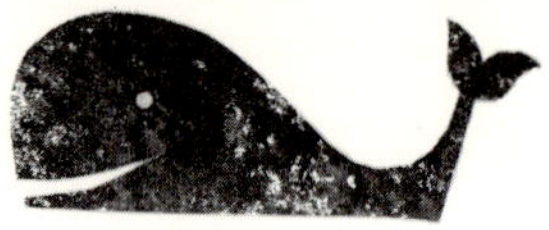

The festivities lasted 'til half past three
When Mot turned about
And headed out
To sea.

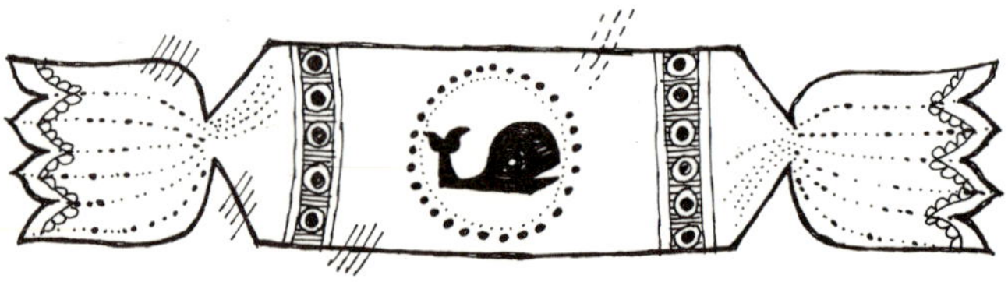

From the Children's Hospital
High above Atwater
At the close of Christmas Day
Halibut York watched them go.
The nurses brought her supper tray
And saw their quiet Eskimo
Laughing.

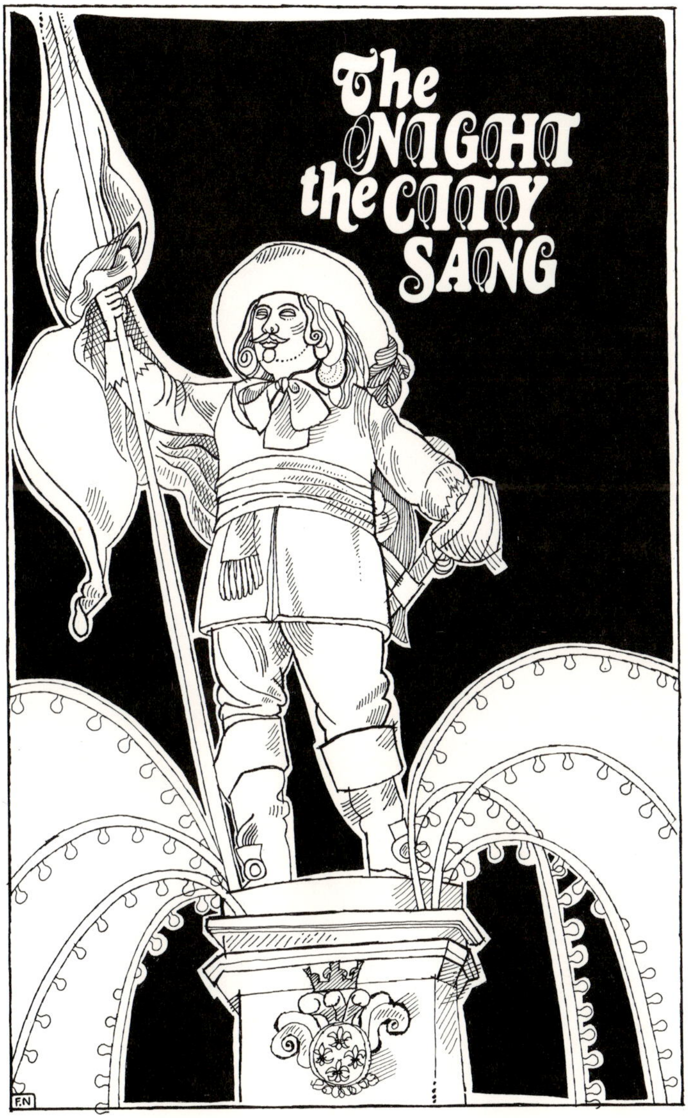
The
NIGHT
the CITY
SANG
F.N

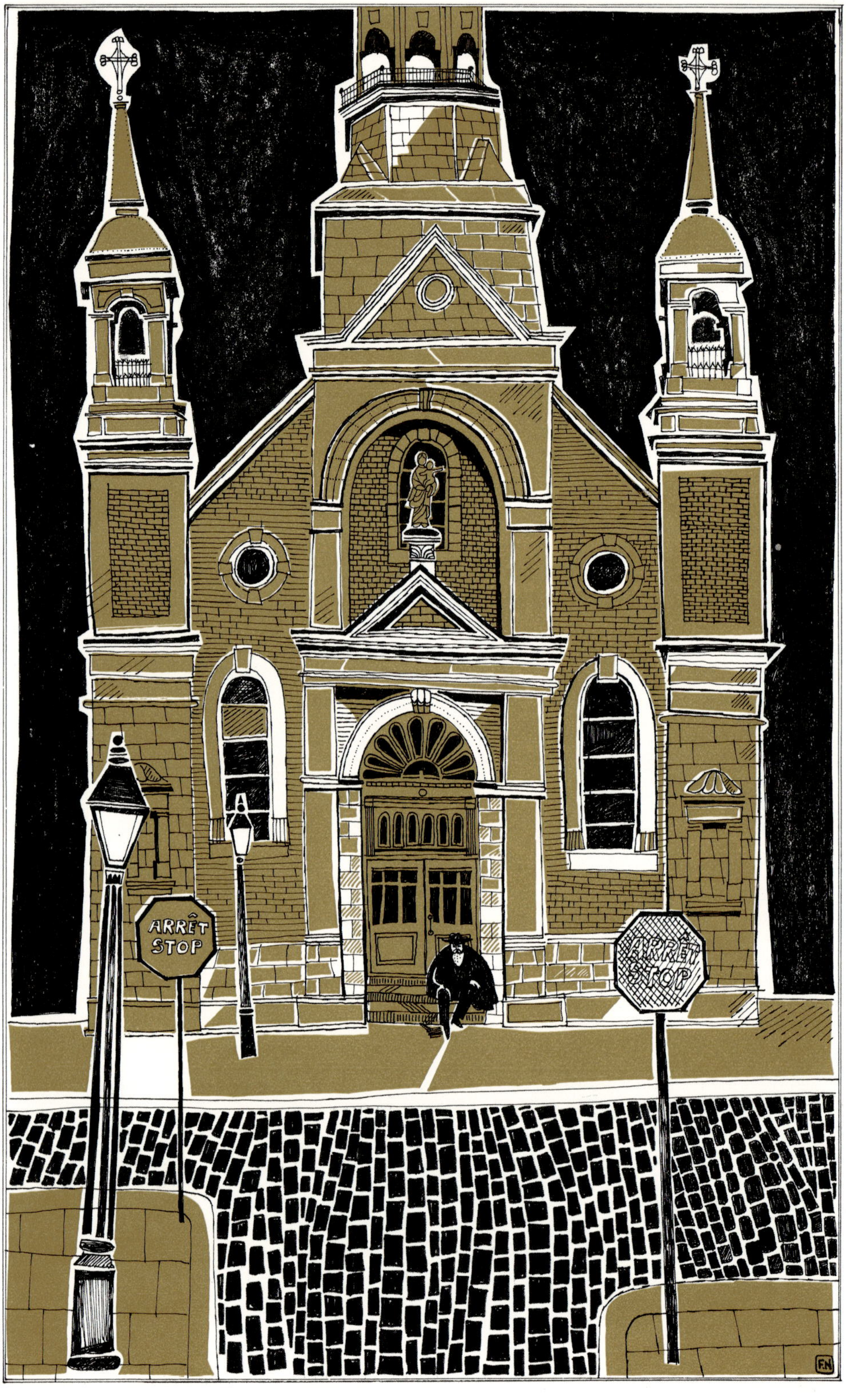
ARRÊT
STOP
ARRÊT
STOP
F.N

Late on Christmas Eve
The old musician sat
On the steps of Notre Dame de Bon Secours
Snowflakes melting on his wide-brimmed hat
Not exactly sure
Why he was there
Too tired to go anywhere else.

Snowflakes sparkled on his cape
Glistened in his beard and hair
Like the halo of lights that flared
Around the Virgin's perch
On the roof of the church.
Lonely as the old musician
The Virgin listened with him
To the sounds of uptown riot
Above the quiet harbour streets.
No tape-recorded carols, no lights,
No children hanging stockings here.
A night like all other nights.

Bonsecours Market dozed with premonitions
Of demolitions and parking lots.
Rasco's Hotel, a warehouse now
(Turnips where Dickens slept)
Remembered how Christmas was kept
A hundred years ago:
Steaming punch in the bar
Le Royer Street a-jingle with sleighs
Those were the wonderful days
In Old Montreal.

Sensing these memories
The old musician raised his head
Filled with distant harmonies
Lifted his eyes to see beauty
In the ancient buildings
Beneath the soot of centuries
Life and a longing to welcome another Christmas.

'My children,' he croaked, 'tonight is not for dying.
'In your empty rooms echoes of music sound
'Remembered carols abound in your silent halls
'Tonight let us quit
'This patate frite century
'And all of you, my children,
'Sing with me!'

Weaving to his feet, he faced the empty church
Grasped an invisible baton
Tapped the swirling snow to command attention;
The storm seemed to catch its breath
As the old musician raised his hand
To summon music.

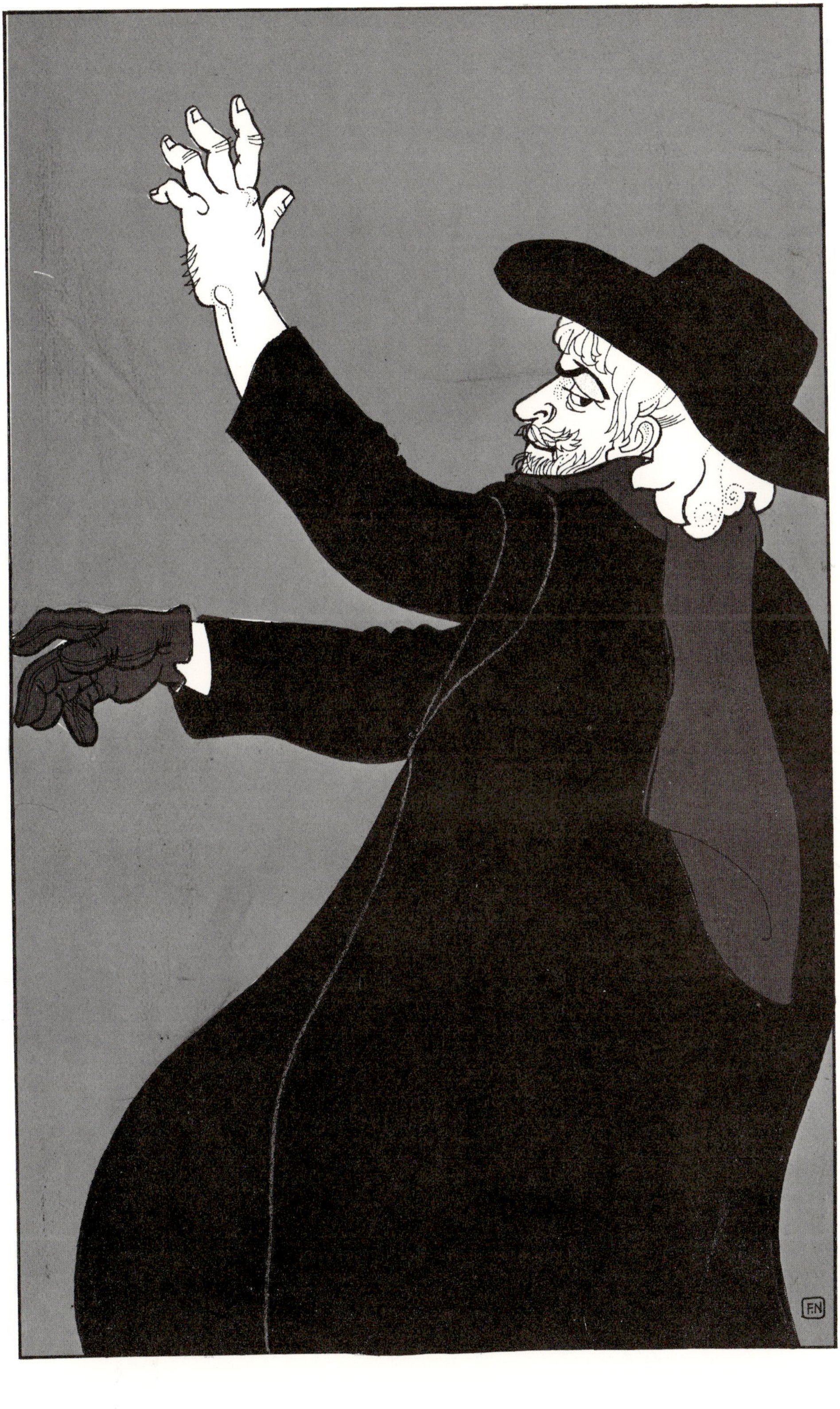
FN

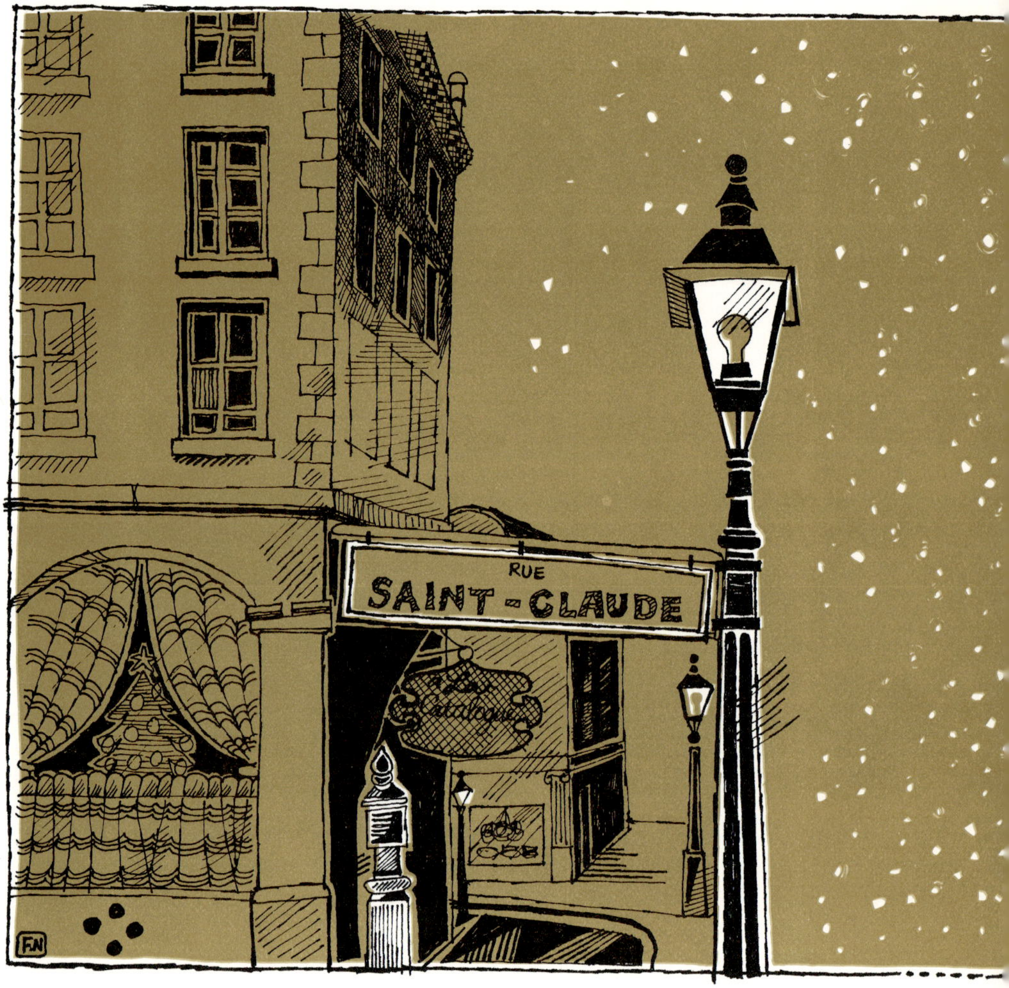
RUE
SAINT-CLAUDE

Within the chapel, the first notes trembled,
Softly from the altar to empty loft
Until, above the chords, within the storm
Warmly joyous, the voice of the Virgin sang.

'Exquisite,' whispered the old musician
And with burning eyes, flinging back his cloak
He waved his hands with remembered grace
To draw a rich bass
From Bonsecours Market.

The Calvet House sounded a silver tone
Papineau's old home added a tenor
With the ringing baritone
Of Rasco's Hotel.
Grain elevators boomed in harmony
Warehouses deliriously carolled
In the steeples of Notre Dame, bells pealed
Maisonneuve reeled on his pedestal above Place d'Armes
City Hall sang with the Bank of Montreal
The old seminary joined Joe Beef's Café
Nothing sacred, nothing tonight profane
The Rodeo shared vocal parts
With the Place des Arts
As the music spread to Craig and along the Main.

The old musician ran, conducted, and ran.
At the end of St. James he paused in the square
Noticing there a demure and silent Queen.
'Your Majesty,' he panted, 'dare I ask why?
'Are we unamused or merely shy?'
Victoria blushed. He raised his hand.
A regal soprano joined the band.

He rushed frantically
Cape streaming in the wind
To Place Ville Marie
Waving his arms like a prophet
He turned the Canadian Imperial Bank of Commerce
To a thin trumpet piercing flying clouds
Royal Bank clashed its aluminum walls
Like cymbals
CIL House was a black cello
Mellow as Casals.
Woodwinds from the Queen E
And timpani in the Archbishop's Palace
John A. Macdonald's tenor panicked his pigeons.

Even Moore's tripartite lady across the street
Formed a resonant bronze trio
And clanged con brio.

People throughout the city were aghast.
They blamed the neighbours, hammered on walls
The police received thousands of calls.
Is it some kind of stunt?
An advertising quirk?
Has Musak gone berserk?
Is it Russia or Cuba?
Good Lord – what was that?
It came from the Oratory
But it couldn't be a tuba!

There was Little Town of Bethlehem
Hark the Herald, Deck the Halls,
McGill led the city in selections
From Handel's Messiah
And not to be outdone – oh no!
The University of Montreal replied
With Bach's Christmas Oratorio
In original French translation.

Amid the pandemonium
A policeman noticed a singular sight:
An old man in cape and sombrero
Flapping like a crow through Ville Marie plaza
Around the lamp standards
Through the pine plantations
Gyrations incomprehensible
And – in the eyes of the law –
Reprehensible.

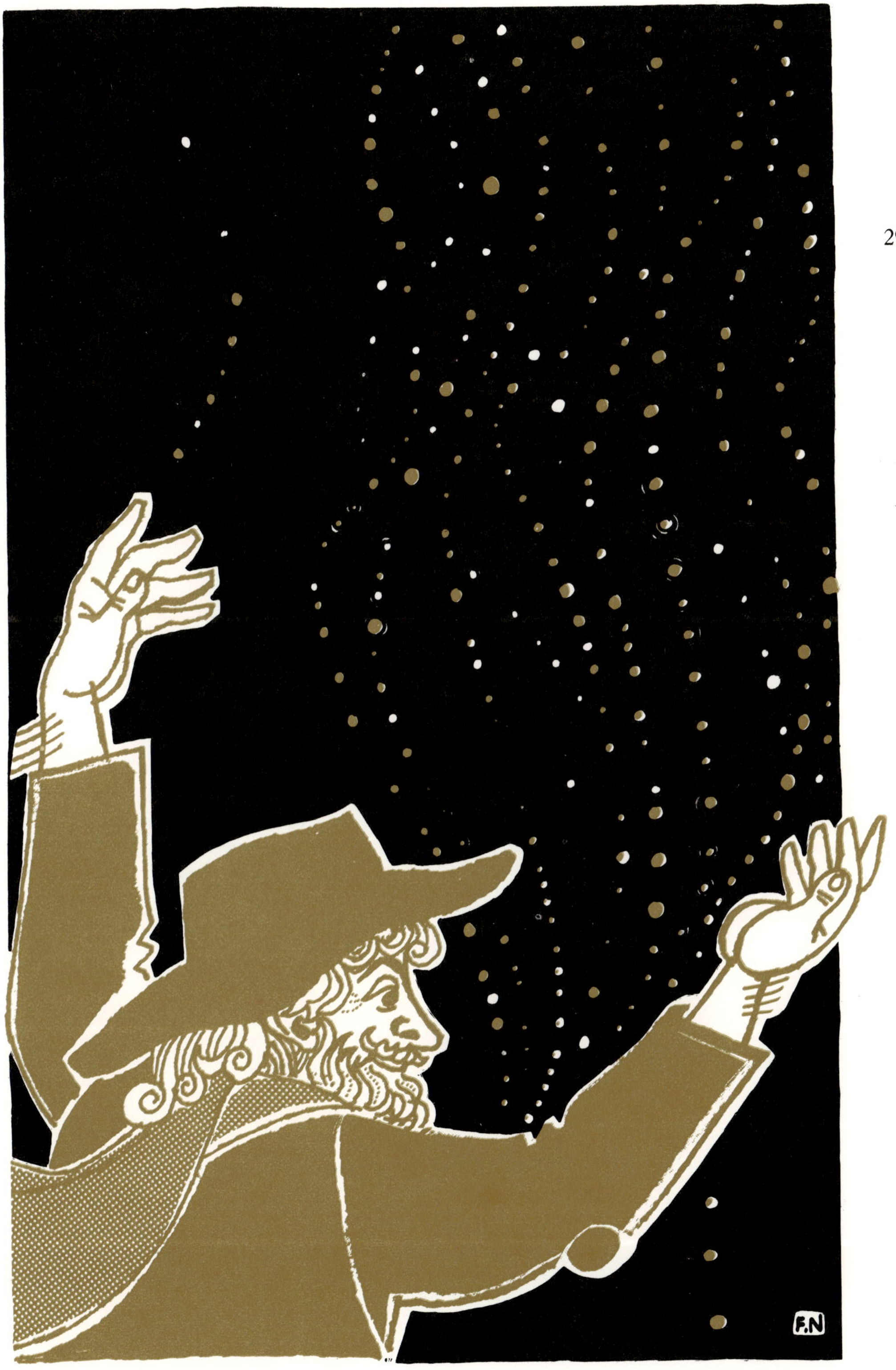
F.N

'Here!' said the policeman
 Collaring the musician
'Come quietly now – no violence.'
And all of a sudden –
Silence.
The music ended
The snow descended
The cop and the musician wended
Their way to a call box.
As the paddy wagon sirened
Through the suddenly silent night
After the hullabaloo
Constable 07482
Glared at the old man
And before long
Much to his annoyance
Burst into song.

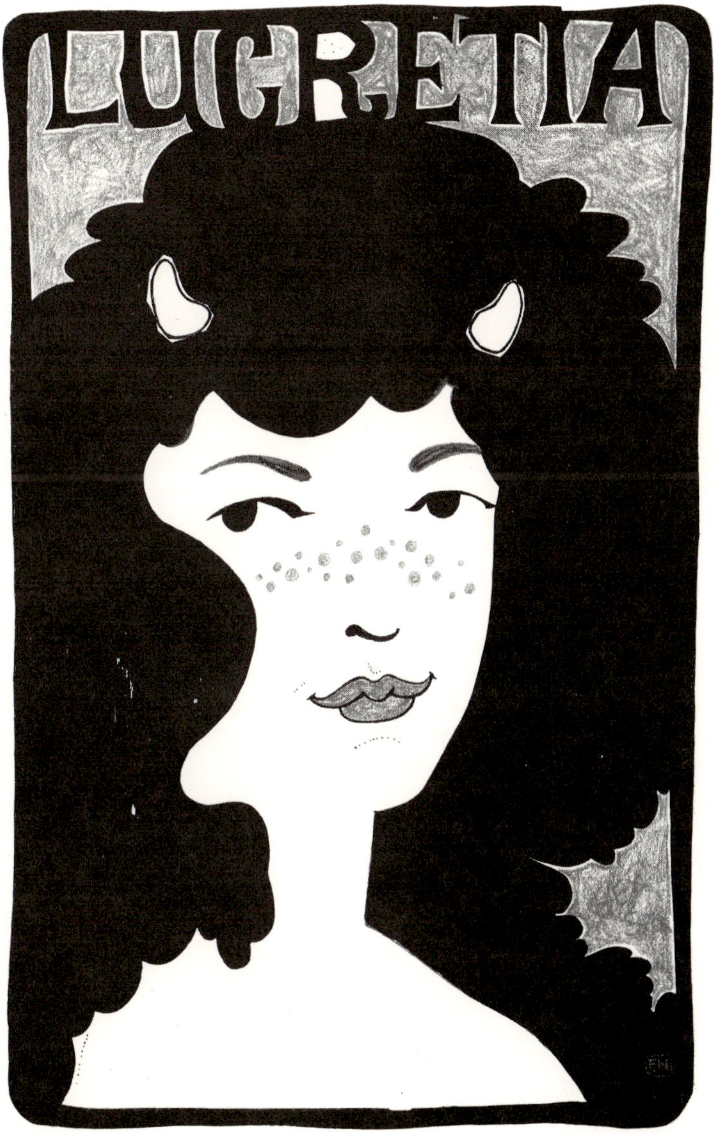
LUCRETIA

Once upon eternity
In the suburbs of infinity
There lived a tiny creature
Called Lucretia.
Her hair was fiery red
The reddest hair in Hades
And her skin, as white as snow,
Unlike the other ladies who
After a millennium or two
Tended to get brittle
And a little charred.
Lucretia just got freckles
Which her sisters found exasperating:
It was wicked to look lovely
When the others were incinerating.

But Lucretia didn't care
And when everyone was cooking
She would make a little face
Entirely out of place and style
A naughty devil's face
That was almost like a smile.
'She's an absolute disgrace.'
Her mother used to say,
'There's a pleasant streak right through her.
'She's a perfect little angel
'Who'll destroy her parents yet.
'We gave her all the worst we had
'And that's the thanks we get!'
But it didn't bother Lou
If no one else could bear her
She knew that she was born to be
A holy terror.

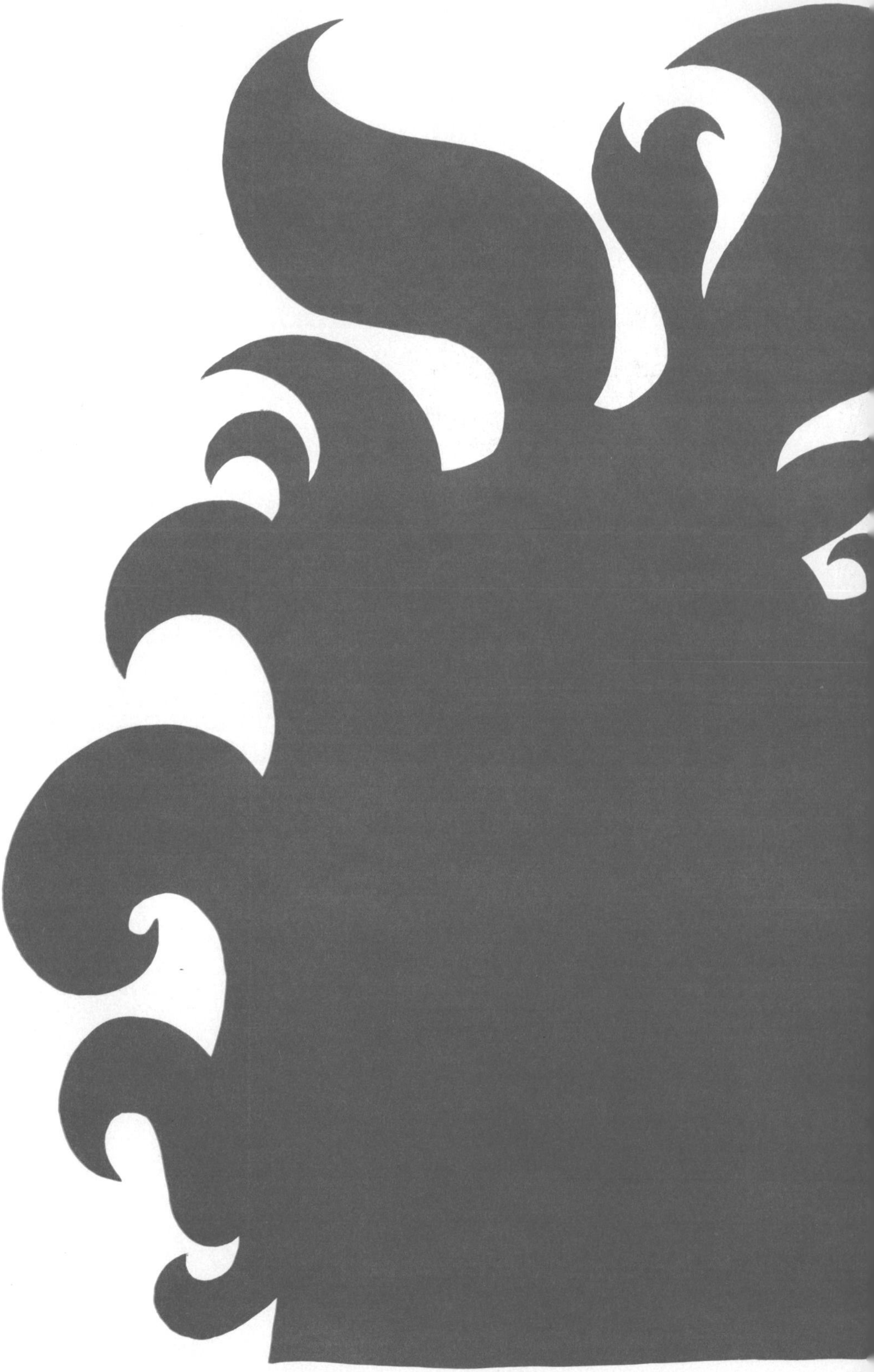

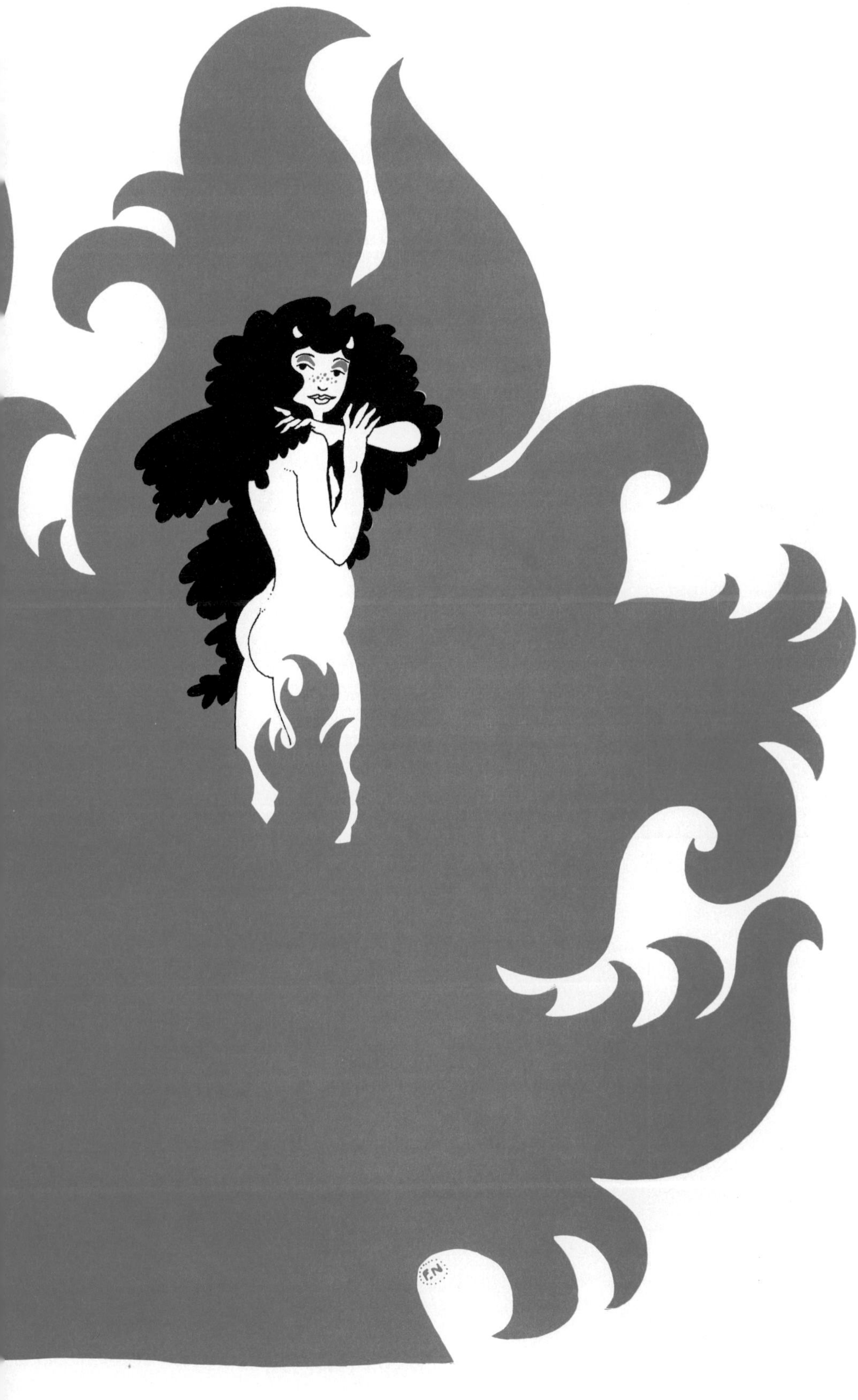

36

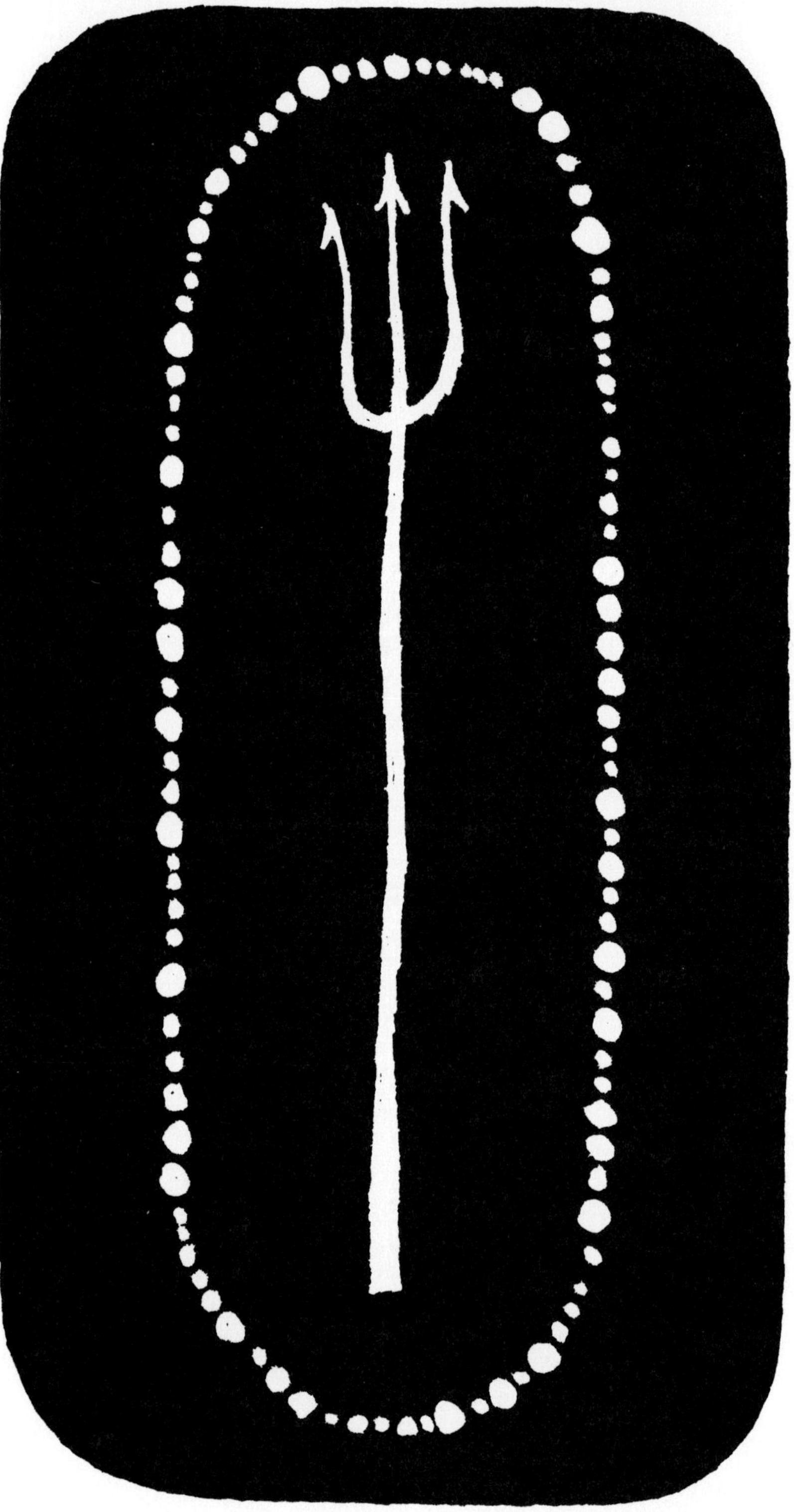

Now every year on Christmas Eve
Hell is locked up tight.
Not even Lucifer himself
Gets out that night.
All the devils stay at home
Resting wing and hoof
While sentries from the Other Place
Patrol the roof.
And every year Lucretia asked
What on earth occurred
But her mother just pretended
That she never heard.

Just before she went to bed
This Christmas Eve, Lucretia said,
That she had left her pitchfork on the lawn.
She ran outside, and ran
As only little devils can . . .
Before her parents knew it
She was gone.

38

At the gates of Hell, Gabriel,
Lord of the Heavenly Host,
Was making toast and tea
Over his flaming sword
When he spied Lucretia
Peering through the bars.
'Please, sir,' she cried,
'I must have missed
'The road to earth in all this smog
'And someone stole my angel's frock
'And please, sir, can't you please unlock
'The gate?'
In nineteen hundred years and more
Of regular Christmas duty at the door
Of Hell, Gabriel had never spied
An angel on the other side;
Nor had he ever seen
A cherub with green eyes
Copper hair
And a certain undeniable
Savoir faire.

'I'm sorry, child,' he said, kindly
'But orders are given to be obeyed
(With a smart click of his wings)
'Blindly!'
'In that case.' Lou proposed,
'I guess I'll have to . . . Say!
'Do you smell something burning?'
'The toast!' cried Gabriel. 'It's black!'
He turned to snatch his flaming sword
And silently, without a word,
Lucretia picked the lock and fled
To earth behind his back.

Hair streaming in the black winds
Of energy that flow through eternity
Lucretia tumbled.
In an instant
She was past the outer galaxies
Hair flickering in the faint
Incredibly ancient rays
Of a million suns spinning
Nights and uncounted days
Like gold and silver threads
Into a shining pocket
Where the small planet Earth
Glows like a glass marble.

Above the earth there were angels
Winging among the Northern Lights
Harping and hymning
And Hallelujahing.
'Out of the way!'
Lucretia's cry
Echoed from space.
The carolling stopped.
Every angel's face was turned
To watch this unidentified object
Barrel into the atmosphere
Helter-skelter in a welter
Of 'Wows' and 'Gollies!'
And inappropriate cries,
Crash through a cloud
And disappear
From sight.
'Another satellite,' they sighed.
'Did you hear the slang?'
'American, for sure.
'It's more than harp and halo
'Can endure.'

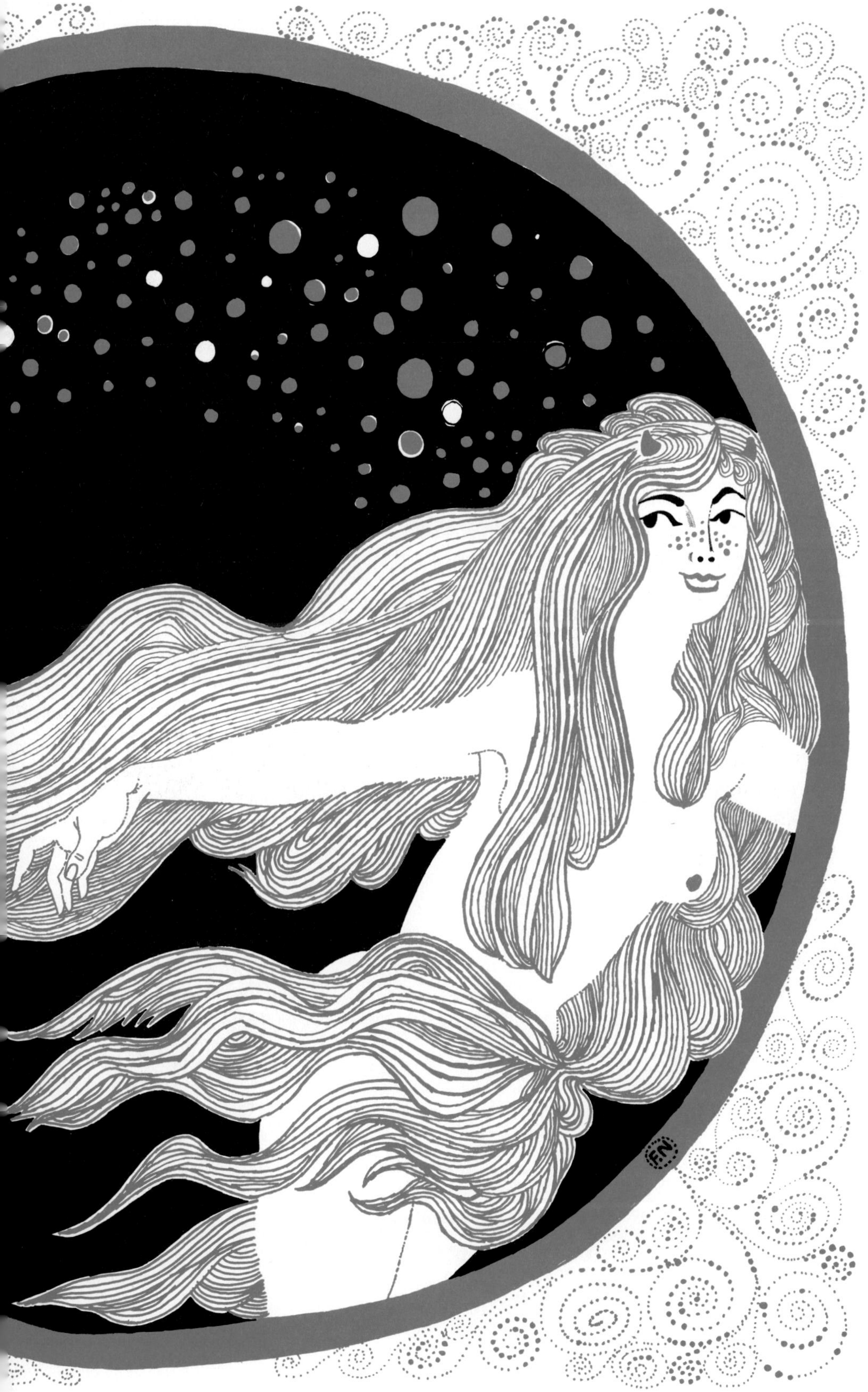

Almost out of control
Diving into Montreal
Lucretia lowered a toe
Into the unfamiliar snow
Went capsizing and pinwheeling
Like a white tornado
Across a yard
And into a fence.
A basement door opened.
An old man peered out
And blinked in surprise.
There she sat, diamonded,
Naked as Eve, spitting like a cat,
And scratching the snow
From her opalescent eyes.

Inside the chill basement room
The old man sat on the edge of his bed
Staring, fingering his beard.
'I must be dreaming,' he said.
'Tell me . . .' commanded Lucretia
Standing beneath the naked light
Like a flaming white Christmas candle.
'Tell me about Christmas!'
'There is nothing to tell,' he said.

But Lucretia persisted:
'How do you make a Christmas?'
'Make it?' said the old man, curiously.
Lucretia asked, 'What's the recipe?'
'Well,' he said, 'first you need a tree.'
'A tree?'
'A Christmas tree, you apparition,
'Bright as fission – an evergreen wigwam
'Arrowed with candy canes
'A bumbershoot blooming with tinsel . . .'
'Like this?' inquired Lou.
She snapped her fingers and cried, 'Olé!'
And . . . zap! (As they say)
The most fantastic Christmas tree
In all the firmament
Sparkled in the basement.

'It's heaven sent' the old man cried.
'Just so,' Lucretia lied,
'Is there anything else that we require?
'If I could have my heart's desire,'
Said the elderly child, his eyes alight,
'I'd like a roaring birch-log fire.
'In a cast-iron stove this Christmas night,
'A bottle of beer, a cat on a rug,
'The smell of turkey and oatmeal stuffing,
'And outside the window –
'White cotton curtains –
'Moonlight on the drifts
'As smooth as milk.
'But that could never . . .
'Well, I never!'

46

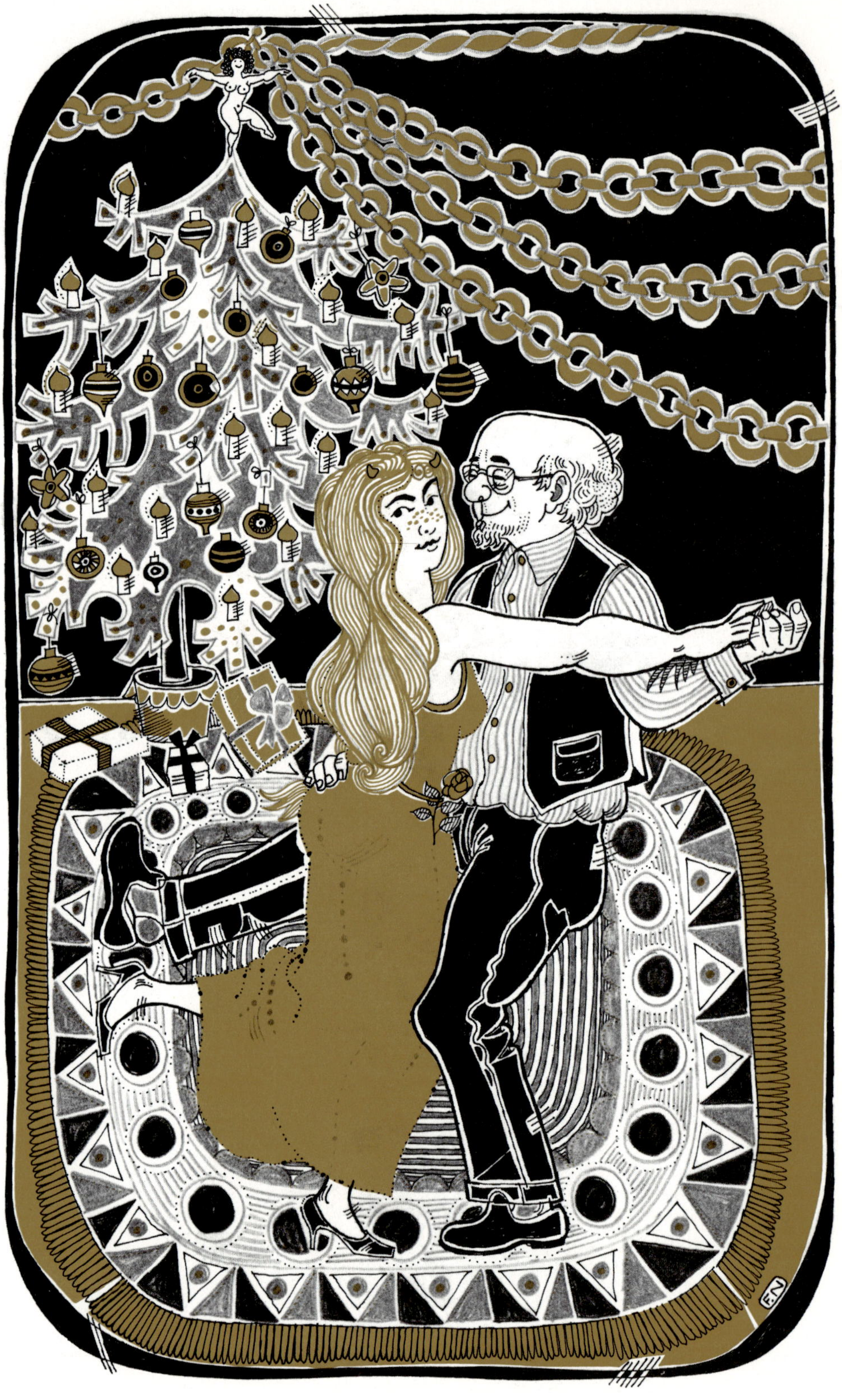

'Let me try,' said the happy old man,
'Here's a party dress for you
'And a hair bow too, velvet green
'Patent leather slippers, socks . . .'
'Why it's gorgeous!' gasped Lucretia,
'Here's a sideboard, Louis Quatorze,
'Persian rugs on all the floors.'
'Don't forget,' the old man cried,
'Holly on the chandelier.'
'We haven't one, you silly dear,'
 Laughed Lucretia as the greenery fell
 All around the Christmas dinner
 That the old sinner
 And the little devil
 Had given each other

 After the feast was over
 After the crackers pulled
 After the paper fortunes read
 When all the world had gone to bed
 It was time for Lucretia to go.
 'Next Christmas?'; the old man whispered.
 'Well,' said Lucretia, 'it's strictly illicit
 'But now that I know
 'What it's all about
 'I wouldn't miss it!'